# Door to Silence

# Door to Silence

John Main

Edited and introduced by
Laurence Freeman

CANTERBURY
PRESS
Norwich

This book is derived from talks given by John Main to weekly meditation groups meeting at his monastery and prepared, recorded and edited by Laurence Freeman.

© Medio Media 2006

First published in 2006 by the Canterbury Press Norwich (a publishing imprint of Hymns Ancient & Modern Limited, a registered charity) 13–17 Long Lane, London EC1A 9PN

Second impression 2008

www.scm-canterburypress.co.uk

British Library Cataloguing in Publication data

A catalogue record for this book is available from the British Library

ISBN 978-1-85311-749-7

Typeset by Regent Typesetting, London
Printed in the UK by CPI William Clowes Ltd, Beccles, NR34 7TL

# Contents

| | |
|---|---|
| *Introduction* | vii |
| *Biography of John Main* | xiii |
| *How to Meditate* | xvi |
| | |
| Peace | 1 |
| Purity of Heart | 7 |
| We Possess the Mind of Christ | 12 |
| The Vision of Unity | 16 |
| Experiencing Tradition | 20 |
| Contacting the Centre | 25 |
| The Aim of Meditation | 29 |
| Unity and Union | 33 |
| Creative Energy | 37 |
| The Context of Meditation | 41 |
| Truth | 45 |
| Time and Reality | 50 |
| Levels of Distraction | 54 |
| The Ordinary Shot through with the Extraordinary | 59 |
| Liberty of Spirit | 63 |
| Open to the Moment of Love | 68 |

Learning to Expect Nothing                              71

Everything that Is One                                  77

Being Present Now                                       81

Hope                                                    85


*Bibliography and Recorded Talks*                       89

*About The World Community for Christian Meditation*    91

# Introduction

The great third-century Christian teacher Origen expressed an understanding of prayer that the readers of John Main will recognize as underlying his contemporary teaching on meditation. 'We do not pray,' Origen said, 'to get benefits from God but to become like God. Just praying itself is good. It calms the mind, reduces sin and promotes good deeds.'

If you have just read those words of Origen in any way deeply, you probably paused to think about them and to re-read them. Their conciseness and precision invites a finer quality of attention from us than we usually give to what we read. The words are carefully chosen, simply expressed and yield insights that are satisfying to the heart's hunger for truth and spiritual knowledge.

This is also the way John Main taught, and the layout of his words on the pages of this book is meant to make it easier for the reader to taste their meaning and experience their wisdom. This is not a new way of presenting spiritual teaching but is part of an ancient tradition of short 'chapters' on prayer, condensed, pregnant phrases or paragraphs, that are meant not so much for quick consumption as for slow chewing. This is a teaching that is slow food for the soul.

When one attunes to this kind of spiritual teaching a kind of quiet excitement is generated. There is the feeling that mind and heart are touched and blessed simultaneously by an expression of truth at a personal level of evident authenticity. This is wisdom, and John Main's message is that meditation is a way of wisdom that allows us to *taste* (the root meaning of *sapientia*, wisdom) the simple and ever-present truth which we are a part *of* and, in fact, can never be apart *from*.

As a monk John Main understood the meaning of simplicity. It is the essence of the monastic way of life and meditation (*oratio pura* or 'pure prayer') could not be simpler. If you find these teachings difficult to understand – or you do not get the purpose of the repetition which is an opportunity to understand better – it is probably because the simplicity hasn't quite grabbed you yet. We approach meditation, like most things, as very complex and complicating people. It will help both to introduce yourself to meditation and to deepen your commitment to the practice if you learn to read these teachings of John Main slowly and attentively, to chew the short sentences rather than rush impatiently on to finish the chapter.

The insights contained in these teachings are experiential truths rather than conceptual systems. That means that if we get their point we will feel that point piercing our veils of ignorance. John Main taught a radical apophasis – that aspect of prayer that discounts words, images and concepts and leads the silence and stillness of poverty of spirit, which Jesus places as the first Beatitude, the first step in the project of human happiness. Evagrius, a disciple of Origen, concisely described this approach when he said that 'prayer is the laying aside of thoughts'.

Because we belong today to such a cerebral and mind-noisy culture this kind of language can baffle and sometimes even anger us. If we think of prayer at all it is the kind of prayer that stays in the head and does try very hard to 'get benefits from God'. But the logic of all prayer is its evolution into ever greater simplicity which, through the work of pure attention, purifies mind and heart. One of the ways we experience the results of this (which are indeed benefits too) is that we sense a transformation of desire taking place in our lives. 'Do not give your heart to what does not satisfy the heart,' said one of the Desert Fathers. And though that might sound obvious it speaks soothingly to the complex and unhappy desire-driven state of a culture of consumers who are pursuing things they really don't want very much. 'To pass beyond all desire is not to pass beyond hope,' John Main says, encouraging us to brave the process of the purification and let compulsive or unconscious desires gradually slip away from our ways of thinking and feeling.

His sense of wonder at the power of the simplicity of meditation to bring about such deep transformation and liberation shines through every page of this book. When one sees this light of wisdom the simple words of his vocabulary – 're-finding the heart', 'experience', 'harmony', 'stillness' – are re-charged with meaning. If you understand what he is saying in these quite simple terms you will be open to the insight that will lead you into practice. John Main's reason for teaching was not to describe the experience any more than was necessary to lead people to the practice that would itself be their teacher.

This practice, for him, could not be better understood or deepened than by the twice-daily meditation, morning and evening, that he recommended, and by the fidelity to the mantra throughout those two half-hours. Practised faithfully it can be seen as a way to do that 'one thing necessary' that Jesus spoke of to Martha. Poor Martha, that stressed-out, overwhelmed, angry and no doubt horribly self-rejecting friend of Jesus and sister of the mirror-opposite Mary. Martha is our culture's patron saint. Like her we need to think deeply about what Jesus meant: the one thing necessary that must be a simplicity that is all-inclusive and thus capable of integrating the opposites of life.

For John Main the practice of meditation opens us to the experience of being that is the basis of all right action and healthy ways of living. First be, then do. Forget being, and your work, health, happiness and human relationships will all be put out of joint. Harmony will be disrupted. Regain the experience of being and you will be amazed how much more you can do and how much more satisfyingly you will do it. What does the experience of 'being' mean? It is not as esoteric as it sounds. Meditate and learn through practice to let go of the success/failure criteria by which we constantly evaluate all experience and you will slip into being as naturally as a duck into the river. John Main returns often to the need to let go of demands and expectations. Having them does not mean that you have failed. But it is necessary to let go of them and get on with the job without constantly interrupting yourself to see how much you are getting out of it.

So far, so good. For John Main, however, there is a deeper understanding of this contemplative wisdom. In the Christian scriptures, in the life of a Christian community and in the Christian faith that allows us to deal with life's hard mysteries, we find through meditation a way of 'verifying the truths of our faith in our own experience'.

I was once giving a weekend retreat and during it spoke with a young woman, a successful lawyer. She told me how surprised she had been to meet a colleague from work on the retreat. After talking a while about the common interest that they had not known they shared until then, her friend paused and then with a little embarrassment asked her not to mention to anyone at work where they had been that weekend. I asked her why she thought her friend had said this and she replied that she understood her perfectly. If it had been a *Buddhist* meditation weekend, she said, there would have been no problem. But if people at work thought she might be *Christian* it could seriously damage her image.

John Main speaks from a Christian contemplative tradition that gets us beyond this foolish, self-defeating cultural block. I have found for many years and in many parts of the world that his teaching connects healingly with the needs and questions of younger people today in ways that they find helpful and inspirational. Imagine a successful, healthy, good-looking young man who works in finance, who has many friends and great potential, but who suffers secret panic attacks and is interiorly crippled by a vacuum of meaning and an inability to make relationships that satisfy his heart. For him, meditation and Christian faith entered his life through John Main's simple and wise words urging him to begin and to persevere in the daily practice.

Nowhere is the power of simplicity more palpable than in the company of children who are meditating. John Main knew that children can and like to meditate but the institutional verification of his insight has taken many years to happen. Now, in schools and dioceses where his teaching on the mantra has entered into the classroom and into lives at their outset, recognizing the contemplative dimension of prayer affirms the contemplative dimension of life at the age when life's patterns are first set.

These words of John Main are drawn from talks he gave to people of all ages and walks of life who came to listen to his teaching and to meditate with him at the weekly groups that he felt were so valuable an aid to people's spiritual journey. Holding the book in your hand the reader can now meet these words with an even greater attentiveness, patience and depth of perception. Wait before forming an immediate opinion. Listen to the words, not to yourself at this stage. Return and repeat. Then, like the Australian aborigine initiating someone into their mysteries, ask, 'What do I hear?' And then, if you have really listened, you will be well equipped to go into the practice itself.

Laurence Freeman

# Biography of John Main

John Main, one of the spiritual masters of our time, was born into an Irish family in England in 1926. He served briefly in the Royal Corps of Signals at the end of World War Two and then embarked on a period of training in religious life. Deciding it was not the time for vows he studied law in Ireland and then joined the British Diplomatic Service.

He was introduced to meditation while posted in Malaya, and began to integrate its practice into his Christian prayer. He returned to Europe and became Professor of International Law at Trinity College Dublin. In 1958 he became a Benedictine monk at Ealing Abbey in London and was advised to give up his practice of meditation; he complied, only to return to it, as he said in his autobiographical *The Gethsemani Conferences*, 'on God's terms not my own' some years later.

He studied in Rome during the heady years of the Second Vatican Council and then returned to teach at the monastery's school in London. In 1969 he was sent to St Anselm's Abbey in Washington DC and here, through John Cassian and the Christian monastic desert tradition, he reconnected to the path of meditation. Increasingly conscious of the importance of this tradition of contemplative prayer for modern Christianity and the world, he formed a small lay community committed to its practice in community and integrated with traditional Benedictine monastic life.

At the invitation of the Archbishop of Montreal in 1977 he formed a new kind of Benedictine community of monks and lay people, based on the practice of Christian meditation and committed to teaching it as its primary work. His talks and retreats during the next period of his life formed the basis of his enduring influence on the spiritual life of contemporary Christianity. In *World into Silence* he wrote a powerful and concise explanation of the meaning of Christian prayer in contemporary terms, true to the theological and mystical traditions and yet able to connect with the spiritual questions and searching of his time. His letters to the growing worldwide community of Christian meditators (*Monastery Without Walls*) opened up new dimensions of spiritual meaning within the tradition and in dialogue with other faiths. Through the spoken word in particular, such as his weekly talks at the monastery recorded as the *Communitas* series, his influence is still powerful in the formation of Christian meditation groups throughout the world. He died in Montreal on 30 December 1982.

*Door to Silence*

# How to Meditate

Sit down in a posture that is comfortable but alert, keeping the back straight. Close your eyes lightly. Breathe normally. Then silently and interiorly begin to repeat a single word or short phrase – your mantra. An ideal Christian mantra is 'Maranatha'. It is the oldest Christian prayer – in Aramaic, the language of Jesus – and means 'Come Lord'. Do not, however, think about the meaning of the word as you repeat it. In fact let go of all thoughts, words and images. As you become distracted from the mantra, simply, gently, faithfully and attentively return to the saying of it. Listen to the word as you say it in four equal syllables: Ma ra na tha.

Meditate for about 30 minutes each morning and evening.

You may find that the support of a group or community is invaluable for the journey you are making. You can contact The World Community for Christian Meditation, founded by John Main, at www.wccm.org. For further information please see page 91.

# *Peace*

M editation is a way of peace and a way to peace. St Paul located the personal source of peace in the persona of Christ:

> Your world was a world without hope and without God. But now in union with Christ Jesus you who once were far off have been brought near through the shedding of Christ's blood. For he is himself our peace.

> *Ephesians 2.12–14*

In this wisdom of the New Testament peace is one of the essential qualities of human existence.

We need to understand what peace means. Yet it is beyond understanding and so to enter into this peace we must enter into the experience of meditation itself.

Meditation takes us to that place beyond understanding where mystery is known and knows us. We cannot understand this outside the experience of meditation and what it shows us.

The Christian tradition and the Christian mystery summon each of us to infinite riches. These riches are personal in Jesus. He is the universal Redeemer; inclusively, not exclusively, by love alone.

Jesus does not condemn anyone. Everyone is eventually redeemed by the universal love that flows from him personally. To be redeemed is not to enter an exclusive club. It is to be thrown open to the universe. It is to be made free from all our chains of fear, of guilt.

We are made free only when we are liberated in the depth of our spirit. Peace is found in this depth of freedom.

Peace is not static. It is full of vitality. It is the sense of joyous well-being that floods us when we find ourselves to be truly harmonious. Every part of our being is in harmony with all being.

By persevering in meditation we find that peace is life finding its own inner coherence. That is a necessary first step.

But it is more than that. Everyone is summoned to find it: if only we become its disciples, disciples of peace. In meditation we find our full resonance in God.

As a monk I have to say to you that no one should be content to live their life at less than their full potential. Each of us must live at 100 per cent of our potential. This is what finding our resonance with God means.

We are called to be resonant not only with God, but in God. This is our call. Our destiny is to find peace beyond our narrow selves in God.

The temptation for modern people is to see peace as a state that can be induced. Our culture persuades us that we can induce any emotional state we choose by chemical means or by changing external conditions.

Peace is not induced. It is entered. It is released. It is not commanded but received. Peace depends on a complete correspondence between all our faculties. All our potentialities need to be awakened if we are to be at peace.

The peace we want to see spreading in the world cannot be imposed by force. You can force a person to put down his gun if you have a bigger gun. You can't force anyone to be peaceful.

If you force your enemy at the point of a gun to pretend to be peaceful you have defeated him. He may develop a secret weapon. You will then always live in fear that he may become stronger than you one day and defeat you.

We can know no peace if we do not exercise gentleness. Peacemakers must be at peace with themselves.

Only peace makes for peace. The only power that can create peace in our world is the power of peace found, known and experienced in human hearts.

This peace power is the core and foundation of our being.

Once found in us this peace is invincible. It is stronger than violence and wiser than fear because peace is creative. It is patient. It knows how to suffer, whereas violence is impatient and destructive.

These truths we must verify not in words but from personal

experience. We cannot find peace within ourselves by using violence against ourselves.

We can't run off our fears, our self-rejection, our anxieties, our repression, our insecurities, by any sort of violence. We come to freedom, to fullness of life only by drinking deep from the fountain of life.

That fountain of life is found springing up in our heart. The fountain of life is a fountain of love.

The word of Jesus to each human being is that we must love our neighbour as we love ourselves. We must love our enemies as we love ourselves.

In this vision peace is not just an impersonal state. It is embodied in a person. Jesus himself is our peace.

Love in this same vision is not just a feeling or emotion. It too is a person. God is love.

Self-knowledge is the universal way to know this person who is peace and love.

In meditation we enter God. We become one with God in our heart. It is not trying to possess God. We are not telling God what we want God to do. Prayer is more than that.

It is becoming one with God in the process of becoming fully ourselves.

Let me remind you again of the importance of the discipline itself. When we meditate we sit still. Stillness of body is very important.

To sit still is the first step away from egoism, from all self-centred concerns.

Then close your eyes gently. Begin to say your mantra, your word. Maranatha. Don't think. Don't think about the mantra or about yourself. Don't think about progress.

Say the word selflessly; continue to say it. As you say the mantra you descend into areas of simplicity in yourself that you hardly suspected were there.

You recover areas of humility in yourself that you thought you had lost.

You regain the capacity to be childlike. To be trusting. To leave all cravings, all desires, behind.

Continue to say your word for the whole time of the meditation. Return to it when you let it go. Don't bother about distractions. Just keep saying your word. It will lead to peace.

To learn to meditate all that is necessary is to return to this experience each day of your life, every morning and every evening.

There are no short cuts. There is no instant mysticism. But there is, for each of us, the infinite love of God welling up in our hearts. That is more than sufficient.

The personal experience of meditation underlies the universal teaching of the gospel.

So he came and proclaimed the good news: peace to you

who are far off, and peace to those who are near by; for through him we both alike have access to the Father in the one Spirit.

*Ephesians 2.17–18*

That's why we meditate: because we have access to the universal source in the oneness of the spirit.

# *Purity of Heart*

Meditation is the way of peace. It is also the way to purity of heart.

> Happy the pure of heart: they shall see God.
>
> *Matthew 5.8*

Purity of heart is a wonderful teaching. It emerges early in the living tradition of those who followed the way that is Christ.

The early teachers of the monastic movement saw that purity of heart is necessary for realizing the purpose of the Christian life.

The meaning of life is to see God with absolute clarity. Meditation is the way to that clarity of vision. The skill we have to learn is to see clearly, purely, what is here.

God, I Am, is here.

The vision of God is not the result of moral striving. It is not the result of an ambitious pursuit of holiness. It is a pure gift of God.

Jesus said:

> You have already been cleansed by the word I spoke to you.

*John 15.3*

The word is the word of God which means God's real presence in our midst. Seeing this active presence is the source of holiness.

So we can forget about our own holiness and simply be open to that presence. At the source-spring of holiness is our always deepening faith in the vitalizing, energizing presence of God in our hearts.

Jesus speaks of holiness as an accomplished fact at this level of being. It does not depend on external achievements but interior awakening.

> No one who has taken a bath needs washing, he is clean all over. You too are clean.

*John 13.10*

We need to realize that we are clean. Purity of heart is ours as a gift. Not to see this is impurity, sin. We are made clean by the personal love of Jesus for each of us.

How can meditation help? It helps by leading us to concentration. Purity of heart is focused, sharp vision. As we say the mantra we narrow down our concentration to the single point of the mantra. That single point leads to this clear vision of God everywhere.

Everything else – all distractions, all thoughts about ourselves, all the ego – has then been put aside. Our vision is concentrated wholly and completely ahead into the mystery, into the vision of God.

We are not looking at God. We are seeing God because God sees us and draws us into the divine self-knowledge.

The secret is learning to come down to that single point. It is like the very wonderful experience of polishing a brass table. A few years ago someone gave me a brass table but it was black, like ebony. If I polished it with wide, broad strokes I wouldn't have got very far but I would have used a lot of polish. The secret is to concentrate on one, small, select point at a time. Then out from this point the whole brass table begins to glisten, to shine. It is restored to its true nature.

Purity of heart is seeing our true selves. The interior clarity to which this summons us is not less than the presence of Jesus reaching towards us in our truthfulness.

The peace we find is his being and his love. I would mislead you if I didn't put this meaning before you as clearly as I can.

The purification that leads to purity of heart leads us on further into his presence within us. It is a consuming fire. Meditation is entering that fire that burns away everything that is not real.

It rubs away all that is not true. It consumes everything that is not loving.

We must not be afraid of the purifying fire. We must have confidence in the fire because it is the fire of love. The fire is the great mystery of our faith. It is the fire *who* is love.

Jesus warns us of this process of purification:

> I am the vine, and you the branches. He who dwells in me, as I dwell in him, bears much fruit; for apart from me you can do nothing. He who does not dwell in me is thrown away like a withered branch . . . If you dwell in me, and my words dwell in you, ask what you will, and you shall have it. This is my Father's glory, that you may bear fruit in plenty and so be my disciples. As the Father has loved me, so I have loved you. Dwell in my love. If you heed my commands, you will dwell in my love, as I have heeded my Father's commands and dwell in his love.

*John 15.4–10*

To live our lives fully there is only one thing we have to do. When we have done it everything else falls into place.

What we have to do is to dwell in love. The mantra roots us in love.

Dwelling in love brings us to purity of heart and clarity of vision. Life is then transformed. Ultimately this process takes us beyond ourselves into the mystery of God and deep into the Trinitarian mystery.

This is the path on which we meditate.

It is often helpful to let music lead you into meditation and the purpose of the music is to forget all the words and thoughts we've been caught up in.

Let them empty out of your mind. When you start to meditate, take a couple of deep breaths to calm yourself. Then spend a moment or two finding a comfortable posture. The essential rule is to keep your spine as upright as possible and to sit still. Then interiorly, silently, in your heart, say your mantra, *Ma-ra-na-tha*, and keep repeating it faithfully.

If you find your mind distracted and wandering in thought, words or imaginations return to the mantra, and keep returning to it.

# We Possess the Mind of Christ

S t Paul taught:

> This is the will of God, that you should be holy.
>
> *1 Thessalonians 4.3*

I was once speaking to some people who knew nothing about meditation and, I sensed, had no real interest in it. I think they were only talking about it for my benefit. But perhaps they were trying to understand it and so they asked, 'What happens in meditation?' One said, 'I should have thought that if you were not thinking of anything, if your imagination isn't working and if no rational process is going on, you would be unconscious.'

Hearing this I understood better why people can find meditation strange and hard to comprehend.

I described the way to meditate. Simply take a word – the word I suggest is '*Maranatha*' – and repeat it over and over again. Listen to it. Attend to it. Sound it. Recite it silently in your heart, continuously, faithfully.

I think they thought it was all some sort of mumbo jumbo. But they asked, 'What happens then? What's the purpose of it? What is the point of it?'

The point of it is this. All the great religious teachers of humanity have spoken of the essential religious experience as perfect freedom, as a complete liberty of spirit. They also describe it as an awakening, a coming to full wakefulness out of illusion.

The point of meditation is coming to full consciousness. This does not mean consciousness of any particular thing, thinking of this or that, but rather full, pure consciousness. Holiness.

St Paul describes this in words I never understood until I had been meditating for some years:

> We, however, possess the mind of Christ.
>
> *1 Corinthians 2.16*

The extraordinary thing is that ordinary people everywhere are called to understand this from their own experience.

Holiness is the point. It means to discover the Spirit of God within us. Wholly open to that Spirit we are taken up into that spirit of love beyond all division. This is not easy to understand or describe. But it is not mumbo jumbo.

To meditate is to exercise the utmost common sense.

To meditate is to sound your rootedness in your deepest reality. Then you cannot be manipulated by anyone else. You will not have to use anyone else's words or thoughts or experiences.

To be wholly conscious, wholly real: that is the call of meditation.

Don't misunderstand me. It is simple, not easy. The way to this is a way of discipline. You must learn to say your word and you must learn to say it with great patience.

The problem for most people today is that the process itself is too simple.

Sit every morning and every evening. Spend about 20 minutes to begin with, then 25, and then get to the optimum period of about half an hour. Every morning and evening simply recite your word.

To begin with don't bother about technicalities. Don't bother about sitting in the lotus position or breathing specially. The rule of posture is an upright spine. Sit upright either on the floor or in a chair. Just breathe, and say your word. When thoughts come or feelings arise, return to the word. Keep saying it in utter simplicity, but also in utter faithfulness. When you realize that you are not saying it, return to saying it.

Whether this process takes you two weeks, two years or 20 years to learn doesn't matter. All that matters is that you are on the way. You are on the pilgrimage to perfect freedom of spirit. Total liberty. You are treading the path of wakefulness, to pure consciousness. You are piercing the veil of self-consciousness.

This freedom means that you are not trapped within yourself. The way ahead is always oneness with God, in Jesus, through the Spirit.

The challenge, as Jesus indicates, is that this way is so simple:

Whoever does not accept the kingdom of God like a child will never enter it.

*Mark 10.15*

I was speaking to these people and I write to you now from a spiritual tradition that goes back thousands of years. It has been followed in the last 2,000 years by Christian men and women who became holy by following it into the mind of Christ.

Holy means fully human. It means compassionate, gentle, forgiving, understanding, and, above all, filled with joy.

Joy flows from holiness rooted in the fact that we have discovered ourselves.

In purity of heart we have actually seen our true likeness to God who is love.

# The Vision of Unity

The beauty of the Christian vision of life is its vision of unity.

The early Christians were the first to understand from the life and death of Jesus that the cosmos and all humanity is united with the One; united with Jesus who is in union with the Father.

The attractive beauty of the Christian vision has always been that this is not an abstract vision. It is also physical. The first teachers saw that all matter, all creation, is drawn into a single, unifying, cosmic movement.

It is a cosmic wave of unity leading us right into the union that is the Divine harmony itself. The call is not to respond to an abstract vision of what might be but to what is.

The human vocation identified by the Christian experience is a call to very deep personal joy. In the great design of human destiny each is brought to fulfilment in the whole.

The thrill of our joy is that we perfect one another. And we bring that perfection to God to mirror God's own infinite perfection.

It is in this cosmic union alone that we finally become ourselves. Without this vision we cannot be called his disciples. It is the great work of each of us to grow into this vision.

Each of us is summoned to do this in our own way and in personal experience. Seeing with our own eyes. Hearing with our own ears. Loving with our own hearts. In him and one with him.

This means going beyond all types of dualism: division within ourselves and division between us and (what seems) outside us.

The overcoming of dualism is transcendence. It is going beyond ourselves.

In meditation we do this: we transcend all the barriers that separate us from ourselves, from others and from God. We go definitively beyond all these false dichotomies that can only be resolved in union, in love, in God.

In other words, each person is summoned to a fundamental simplicity. Each must learn just to be.

This is the call of deep prayer for which we feel a soul-hunger. We long to be in love. In trust and in fearless openness to what is. To God who is love.

As we open the eyes of our heart to this vision it can be very intoxicating. So we need to approach it with humility. To be humble is to be truly rooted in what is.

To be humble each must renounce power and force. We must become not only humble but also meek.

17

The only power we can trust absolutely is the power of Jesus who humbled himself. His power is the power of pure love. If we are open to it, it propels us into selflessness, towards otherness, into love.

It is the power that enables us to know and love ourselves. Then, to know and love others. It is also the power that allows us to be known and to be loved.

Each of us is called to discover that this power is to be found in our own hearts. This humility is found in our own hearts.

The only condition necessary is that we seek for it above everything else. The seeking takes us beyond all compromise, beyond insecurity, beyond fear. The challenge is real. Will we respond to what is? Or will we stay asleep in the nether world of fear and illusion?

Our call is to be the uniquely loveable person that God has created us to be. Our call is to be real. Our call is to be free. To enter into that total liberty of spirit that is the hallmark of the Christian. Our call is to be.

This is the call we respond to each day of our lives as we meditate morning and evening. To be open to what is essential. To be open to what endures. To be open to love.

This call is the cosmic vision of the early Church:

> He rescued us from the domain of darkness and brought us away into the kingdom of his dear Son . . . He is the image of the invisible God; his is the primacy over all created things . . . And he exists before everything, and all things are held together in

him. He is, moreover, the head of the body, the church. He is its origin, the first to return from the dead, to be in all things alone supreme. For in him the complete being of God, by God's own choice, came to dwell. Through him God chose to reconcile the whole universe to himself, making peace through the shedding of his blood on the cross – to reconcile all things, whether on earth or in heaven, through him alone.

*Colossians 1.13–20*

Our response to what has been achieved in Christ is to open our hearts to this supreme reality.

# Experiencing Tradition

The first challenge in responding to the call is just to understand how simple it is.

However, we live in a highly complex society. Everyone has to deal with a multiplicity of problems each day, each of them complex. It's very difficult to believe that anything is simple, straightforward or clear. It's hard to believe that such a teaching as meditation could be true and effective.

I teach meditation as a Benedictine monk. So our message as monks to a complex world is simple: we are all the inheritors of a long and rich spiritual tradition. It has been passed on. It has survived for centuries, despite many attacks on it, despite many misunderstandings and despite blatant neglect.

We have been raised in a largely intellectual climate with great dependence on the media. So we tend to think that once something has been written down it has an automatic power to survive on its own.

But a tradition cannot survive either by being talked about or because it has been written down. It survives only when it is practised.

A tradition survives and grows only when men and women can be found who will enter into the *experience* of the tradition.

We not only inherit a tradition, but we also recreate the tradition in every generation by discovering it from our own experience. At the moment of rediscovery the tradition lives and living it possesses power.

It becomes a living flame that has the power to enlighten, to guide and to warm.

How do we enter into the tradition? Not just by reading the accounts of the great spiritual men and women of the past who knew it. We have to do what they did.

The basic challenge is to let go of our preconceived ideas about what the tradition is. It is about letting go of our ideas about meditation, about the nature of the experience, about God. Then we encounter the tradition in an entirely new, personal and unique way.

By letting go of concepts and images of what it is, we learn to be still, to be silent and to enter the experience directly. If we have the courage to enter this silence we really begin to learn, to appropriate, to be part of the tradition.

It is in silence that we really begin to enter the experience of what it means to be.

When you begin it is essential to understand that meditation is as ordinary as breathing. Meditation is to the spirit what breathing is to the body.

We can then learn to be who we are now and, with great simplicity, to accept who we are. So, don't expect that anything should *happen* when you meditate. Don't imagine your meditation is 'successful' because something happens, or a 'failure' if nothing happens.

Meditation is simply being here and now as we naturally are. It is the process of becoming one and in harmony with the basic energy of the universe. What 'happens' *is* this harmony, this realization.

We don't have to make this harmony happen. It is. We have simply to be. Then we know. Most of us want to know that we are. But the reverse is truer. First be, then you can truly know that you are and what is and what is not.

At first the energy of this realization is potential energy waiting to be released in us. It is realized not by thinking about it or by trying to will its release. It is released simply by opening our hearts and minds to the presence of the energy within us.

Once released the energy transforms us outwards from within. All dimensions of life are affected for the better. With this energy of reality we pass through the veils of doubt, confusion and illusion.

We pass through the wall of the ego into the infinite space and freedom of God.

Meditating is not only simple, it is simplicity itself. Sitting still teaches us this. Stillness is the first step on the journey of self-transcendence.

Once you are sitting quite still allow your face muscles to relax.

Sometimes when people are beginning a meditation, the most colossal frown appears on their face which seems to say, 'I'm going to meditate if it kills me.'

The point, however, is to be completely relaxed. Then you begin to say, silently, interiorly, your word, your mantra. The mantra I recommend you to repeat continuously is '*Maranatha*': four equally stressed syllables, Ma-ra-na-tha. And that's the work for the 20, 25 minutes or 30 minutes of the meditation session.

Sit still. Sitting still is important because it prepares for stillness of spirit. Meditating is complete unity of body and spirit. Close your eyes gently. Be quiet in body and spirit. Let go of thoughts. Let go of your imagination. Let go of your ideas. Don't be concerned about what you are thinking about yourself or what others may be thinking about you.

To meditate you need great simplicity, the simplicity of an unself-conscious child. Meditating is returning to the innocent source of our being. We return to ordinary life refreshed and renewed, more childlike, by our encounter with the source. The way is the way of the mantra.

The art of saying your mantra is to learn to listen to it. So, as you say it, silently and interiorly, without moving your lips, listen to it. Listening to the sound of the mantra is the way into the silence, the work of silence.

The cycle of birth and death is held in this silence:

> Jesus answered: 'In truth, in very truth I tell you, unless a man has been born over again he cannot see the kingdom of God.' 'But how is it possible', said Nicodemus,

'for a man to be born when he is old? Can he enter his mother's womb a second time and be born?' Jesus answered, 'In truth I tell you, no one can enter the kingdom of God without being born from water and spirit. Flesh can give birth only to flesh; it is spirit that gives birth to spirit. You ought not to be astonished, then, when I tell you that you must be born over again.'

*John 3.3–8*


We are born again, the tradition is born again, in the silence of the spirit.

# Contacting the Centre

To reach the source of our being we take a first step over and over again.

The step, when we understand this as a Christian way of prayer, the repeated first step is to find ourselves.

St Augustine puts it like this:

> We must first be restored to ourselves and then making of ourselves, as it were, a stepping stone we rise thence to God.
>
> *Retractions 1(8)3*

The first step is to discover our own deeper reality, our essential being. To many people today this might seem to be the ultimate goal too. But in the experience of prayer, once this first step has been taken, we are swept beyond ourselves into the infinite mystery that is God.

Self-knowledge leads inevitably to the knowledge of God.

All that is needed is honesty, integrity. Honesty to know ourselves. The power of integrity, the wholeness which self-knowledge brings, to complete the journey beyond ourselves.

Meditation is the journey into the otherness of the other. Divine integrity can only be encountered through the portal of our own integrity.

This is important to state because religion can so easily avoid honesty and dispel wholeness. We can be so busy with rituals, creeds, religious claims of priority, external observance, enforcing conformity rights, that we forget the first step into honesty and integrity.

When we lose the quality of openness everything is lost. We have lost faith.

How can we recover what we have lost? How can weak, fallible, egocentric beings come back to integrity? The energy necessary for this journey of rediscovery is given to us: grace.

Grace is found within every human heart, however clouded that heart may have become. The tradition of Christian prayer teaches us that we are irresistibly and continuously summoned back to the centre of being through re-finding our heart.

We are summoned to the centre by the centre. Basic Christian theology teaches us that the whole mystery of the Trinity is being lived out in the centre of each human person.

Because the Trinitarian dynamo is the dynamic of all reality, once we make contact with our centre we also connect with every centre because we make contact with God.

God is the centre of all that is.

Through the daily pilgrimage of meditation we begin to live from conscious rootedness in that centre. We are stabilized by the centredness of reality itself. The marvel of the Christian vision and the Christian experience is that this Trinitarian dynamo is the love of God.

It is a love that is at the same time annihilating and creative.

Why do people often draw back from meditation as they draw back from love? Why can people cling to an infantile level of prayer and prefer to stay in immature egotistical isolation? Because they fear the annihilating aspect of love.

But what is annihilated is only the old self: our illusory self; our selfish, self-centred suffering self. Then we are re-created. We are made into a new creation by the same power of love.

We have to confront the annihilating, the loss of self. People are often repelled by the negative language of the mystical tradition and of the scriptures: surrender, death, loss.

But what is surrendered is what is worthless. What is annihilated is what is unreal. What dies is what is impermanent anyway.

The essential experience of prayer is the powerful surge of God's creative love. It is this surge of love that brings about a break-through into the Kingdom of God. The Kingdom of God is simply the power of divine love released and penetrating into every fibre of our being: the Kingdom of God is within you (Luke 17.21).

The Kingdom transcends the duality of inner and outer. But it is an experience that must be known first from 'within'. The knowing of it harmonizes and integrates us. It becomes conscious through the power of love.

It is known by opening our hearts and minds to the heart and mind, the consciousness, of Jesus. Silence and attention are necessary for this to be realized.

The overcoming of self-consciousness is the work of pure attention. The state of prayer is a state of complete purity of heart. In this state we are wholly open and attentive to reality in its purest and most intimate manifestation.

We are open to the Spirit who is creative love present in the depths of our Spirit. The Spirit of the Creator. The spirit of all creative energy.

Prayer renews and sustains us. It sustains our relationships, our work and all of life. It continually fills us with fresh waves of creative energy. It reveals an infinite expansion of spirit in which we pass beyond the ego's fears and desires into pure and unalloyed oneness.

Total acceptance in total love.

What is required? Simplicity and fidelity. Not demands. Not desire. But humility in self-knowledge, poverty of spirit in non-possessiveness. All this we learn in our daily meditation.

It is what Jesus teaches those who come to him.

> [Jesus] said to them, 'Let the children come to me; do not try to stop them; for the kingdom of God belongs to such as these. I tell you, whoever does not accept the kingdom of God like a child will never enter it.' And he put his arms around them, laid his hands upon them, and blessed them.
>
> *Mark 10.14–16*

# The Aim of Meditation

The most important thing to learn about meditating is how to meditate.

It is extraordinarily simple. And that's the problem. Very few, on first hearing about it, can believe that the simplicity can be so powerful. Sometimes it takes months, even years, to come to terms with the simplicity.

Part of our problem with simplicity is our psychological understanding of self-knowledge. Much of the interest in the spiritual life today has a psychological origin.

People are often interested in what meditation can teach them about themselves. It is easy for us to see everything in terms of self-improvement, auto-therapy and self-understanding.

There is a value in this. But self-fascination can be disastrous for the spiritual journey. There is a danger that after we take up meditation we see that we are understanding ourselves better and then get diverted from self-transcendence to self-fixation.

We will find eventually that we have left the pilgrimage into unitary knowledge and wisdom. We end up stuck in the limited knowledge of our separateness. We become so entranced by our own mental operation that we forget we are on a pilgrimage into the mystery of God.

The essence of the gospel is the essence of meditation: not self-analysis but self-transcendence.

> If anyone wishes to be a follower of mine, he must leave self behind.

Luke 9.23

There is something arduous and demanding about this journey. It requires nerve to take the attention off yourself.

By letting go of ideas and gazing wholeheartedly ahead, the meditator becomes like the eye that sees but cannot see itself.

This is a journey that requires faith and commitment to what is beyond you, to what is greater than you. The journey requires the humility to stop thinking about yourself.

As we advance on the journey we continually let go of what we think we have achieved.

When we start we are concerned with progress, and how perfectly we are doing the techniques. But we learn that we have to let go of the attempt to measure progress. This is the challenge that, in practical terms, means to keep saying the mantra from the beginning of the meditation until the end.

That's something to understand absolutely clearly. To learn to meditate it is necessary to meditate every day, morning and evening. It's necessary while you are meditating to say the mantra from the beginning until the end.

Whatever thoughts come into your mind, whether they are good thoughts, religious thoughts, holy thoughts or bad thoughts, let them all go and say the mantra.

By doing this we avoid the business of rating ourselves in terms of success or failure, even of progression or regression. Meditating is the way of learning just to be; to be who you are now in the presence of God in simplicity. The mantra leads us to this as we learn to be faithful to it.

The gospel calls us, not to analysis, but to synthesis. The synthesis of consciousness, of self, that is spiritual knowledge is the necessary truth to know another. It requires commitment to the other.

You can never know another until you love the other. This requires the simplicity to let go of everything else so that we may love. Then we come to the heart of the mystery, the gnosis, the spiritual knowledge that the New Testament speaks of is not so much our own knowledge, which is always limited, but rather the knowledge by which we are known.

The invitation is to throw open our hearts and minds to know with the knowledge of God. The call of the New Testament is to union in this knowledge that is love. We must first be unified in ourselves in order to find union with God.

The love of God which we discover in our hearts bestows enormous confidence. This confidence is born of the deep humility of knowing ourselves in the knowledge with which God knows us.

So the order of our development goes something like this: saying the mantra with growing faithfulness leads to self-transcendence, inner unity and harmony. Then comes our emergence as a fully coherent person. And then comes deeper relationship with others, self-forgetfulness, transcendence in love, union with God and full consciousness.

The aim of Christian meditation is to enter into full union with the consciousness of Christ.

In the silence there comes peace, interior order and harmony which gradually we recognize as the presence of God.

To begin, learn to let go even of this thought. We learn to let go by saying our mantra, 'Maranatha'. Say it gently, without haste or expectation. Be relaxed about it.

Say it continually.

# Unity and Union

Meditation helps us better understand the ancient myths because it opens us to the deep levels of personal and collective consciousness.

> When the woman saw that the fruit of the tree was good to eat, and that it was pleasing to the eye and tempting to contemplate, she took some and ate it. She also gave her husband some and he ate it. Then the eyes of both of them were opened and they discovered that they were naked; so they stitched fig-leaves together and made themselves loincloths. The man and his wife heard the sound of the LORD God walking in the garden at the time of the evening breeze and hid from the LORD God among the trees of the garden. But the LORD God called to the man and said to him, 'Where are you?' He replied, 'I heard the sound as you were walking in the garden, and I was afraid because I was naked, and I hid myself.' God answered, 'Who told you that you were naked? Have you eaten from the tree which I forbade you?' The man said, 'The woman you gave me for a companion, she gave me fruit from the tree and I ate it.' Then the LORD God said to the woman, 'What is this that you have done?' And the woman said, 'The serpent tricked me, and I ate.'

*Genesis 3.6–14*

33

The journey of meditation into the prayer of Jesus leads to the re-unification of all that has been separated in us and between us and the world as a result of the Fall.

The first step is to be reunited to ourselves. Once we begin to enter our own unity we are ready to go beyond ourselves into union with others, the world and God. Unity naturally expands into union.

Meditation is our way to this unity within ourselves that leads to union with others.

It is the only real basis for union, because unless and until we are united within ourselves we hardly exist as a person capable of relationship. We have not yet learned the self-forgetfulness, the self-giving and the self-commitment that union demands.

We all begin our pilgrimage as divided beings. We are divided between heart and mind, body and spirit. We inhabit a dualistic world. Our conception of reality is fractured.

We begin the pilgrimage because we feel at a deeper than ordinary level that an inner unity exists; that there is a harmonious coherence in ourselves, within ourselves and in all creation.

The core of the problem is that we think of reality as outside us. We see everything, self and others, internal and external, as divided. It is this perception of dividedness that is the root of sin within us. This is the meaning of the Fall as told in the book of Genesis.

Before the Fall there was innocence and free-flowing harmony. After the Fall, there was enmity with others and disharmony

34

within the self. *The Cloud of Unknowing* speaks of meditation as the way to heal the wound of sin in us at its root.

Meditation is the work of healing and of restoration of wholeness at a higher level of development. It is a work of growth, not regression. It is a journey in which we transcend all dividedness. Leaving the dualistic perception of reality we travel in faith into the unity of God.

In Genesis, after the Fall, Adam hides himself when he hears God walking in the garden in the cool of the evening. He is afraid. The basis of all dividedness is fear. Meditation discovers the infinite love in the heart, and love casts out all fear.

The Fall could be seen as the necessary emergence of ego in human development. The ego is the image we have of ourselves, the persona we try to project. Once the ego was unleashed in them, Adam and Eve became self-conscious. Their self-image suddenly required clothes so that they could present themselves in an acceptable way to others and to God.

All disguises, illusions and false perceptions of ourselves and others and of God are spun by the ego. The ego is like a prism. The light of reality passes through it and is refracted. The shaft of pure light is split up into component parts and deflected from its true course.

Meditation dissolves the prism. It reunites the fragmented pure beam of light. It enables us to enjoy the gift of our being without shame and fear, as a whole. It enables us, as sheer gift, to be wholly open to the wonder of God's oneness.

We enjoy oneness, not by observing it from the outside but by entering its centre. The ego always calls us to self-preservation. The true self, the centre, is created for self-transcendence.

All unity has a centre and our unity is found in our own centre, called the heart. In the heart we find the centre of all who is one with all.

The return to the centre (from which we feel we have fallen) is, like our creation itself, the gift of God. We say our mantra by the gift of God and we arrive in God's own time. All we have to do is to dispose ourselves, to make ourselves available.

That we do as we meditate morning and evening. That we do by leaving thought, speculation, ratiocination behind and leaving Eden for an even better world.

# *Creative Energy*

The most important task in life is to live it to the full.

So far as we can we must realize the full potential for being alive. Meditation is integral to this task. It is the process whereby we keep in contact with the creative centre of our being in a constant state of expansion. In this process creative energy is continuously released within us, recreating our original creation.

In our modern secular world, we easily forget that we have a divine origin.

The incandescent energy of our spirit emanates from the Spirit of God. When we forget that God is our Creator we lose contact with our essential nature. Our humanity is thereby diminished. We risk being dehumanized. The great task is to remember our spiritual capacity.

Our potential for creativity is to respond fully to the gift of our existence, to the lives of others and to the giftedness of the whole creation. This means to respond at the point of origination within the Spirit of God.

It is easy to allow ourselves to become dehumanized, to give up and become not citizens but consumers. In our materialistic, technological society it is easy to live with only materialistic goals achieved in a mechanical way. We can go through routines each day having lost the freshness of creativity and freedom.

As a result we live in a rush. One routine follows the next, distracted for an interlude by entertainment or diversion but at heart deadened by the pressures of work or play.

There are two things we can do to break out of this cycle and enter the creative mystery of life. First, we have to stop the rush of activity. We must learn the priority of being. First be then do. We must learn how to be still. That is what our regular times of meditation are for.

Second, we have to learn to be profoundly silent. We must stop the racket going on around us and in our heads. It is easy enough to switch off the radio, the television, the CD player. It is not so easy to switch off the torrent of ideas and images in our heads. This is the purpose of the mantra.

If you truly want to learn to meditate, it takes time and patience to say the mantra, from the beginning of your meditation until the end.

Meditation directly addresses both of these tasks: being still and becoming silent. We *learn* how to be still. We *learn* how to be silent. By learning this we discover how to be in our own place.

Being fully alive requires us to be rooted in our own place, whatever that may mean for each of us. But for everyone the place to be rooted is found within ourselves.

There is nothing that our modern world needs more urgently than men and women who are rooted in themselves, confident of their own being, and confident of their own capacity for goodness. Strong in their capacity for loving and for being loved. For such genuine confidence we need to be wholly at one with ourselves.

Sitting still, every morning and every evening, learn to meditate. Take a minimum of 20 minutes but the optimum time is about 30 minutes. In that practice learn stillness and rootedness.

Once we are rooted and still, we begin the next great task: learning to pay attention. Attentive to the mystery at the heart of creation. Learning to live always in harmony with the mystery.

Our awareness of being is the wonder of life. That awareness is intensified by our awareness of the being of others.

This awareness is always expanding into the awareness of the being of all creation, into our awareness of the being of God. Life reaches its fully human capacity, its most profound centre, when we realize that being is love.

We are alive in direct proportion to our capacity for love and for being loved.

Meditation is simply the process whereby we enter fully into the mystery of life, our life, the life of others, and the life of God.

And who is God? We cannot understand the question or the answer to it outside of the state of stillness and silence.

In the silence we learn reverence: reverence for ourselves,

reverence for others, and reverence for God. In the silence we learn humility: the humility to accept the love of others and the love of God.

> Dear friends, let us love one another, because love is from God. Everyone who loves is a child of God and knows God, but the unloving know nothing of God. For God is love; and his love was disclosed to us in this, that he sent his only Son into the world to bring us life.

*1 John 4.7–10*

Meditation is an entry into that quality and depth of life, rooted in ourselves, rooted in love, rooted in God.

# The Context of Meditation

It is not so difficult to understand the importance of prayer. But what is prayer? The poet George Herbert described prayer as 'the soul's blood'. It is vital to our whole being. But what is the context in which we discover this on the pulse beat of our own experience?

Christians have often tended to privatize prayer, thinking of it as an individual concern and seeing our involvement in community as something quite separate. In the New Testament the central unifying reality of love compels us to see prayer as inseparably personal *and* communal.

The context of prayer is the mystical Body of Christ.

Love of God, love of neighbour, love of ourselves: these are inter-dependent and starting with one we are led to the others.

Jesus is the revelation of God, God's love made visible.

The vision he shared and embodied is of a community whose limits are boundless. Christianity, in this vision, is a community of brothers and sisters of great diversity on a global scale. They respond together to the same reality, however it may be described, that is beyond them and yet contains them. It also constantly expands them.

In meditation we seek to be, to be who we are and to come into the presence of God who is as God is.

Above all, in our prayer we are not trying to possess or to change God. If we are trying to do anything it is to be one with God as he is.

A new, wonderful dimension is added to prayer when we find others – who become friends – with whom we share this experience.

In sharing our meditation together, we accept one another as we are. We are not trying to possess or to change one another. Each of us seeks to *be* to the fullest of our potential.

We know, both from the words of Jesus, and from our experience of him in our hearts, that to *be* is to *be with*, and to *be for*.

The gift of a community growing – because those who live together also pray together – is that we find people to be with and these same people are people with and for us.

Meditation is a way to mature human relationships, relationships that enable us to really rejoice in the being of another.

In place of the wish to possess or control others, there develops a delight in knowing them in their uniqueness.

It's the same with God. We don't need to harass God, to bombard God with words, demanding that he take notice of us how and when we want.

In the simplicity of our humble repetition of the mantra we only seek to be with God, to be here and now for God.

So we learn to rejoice in being in and with God, and more and more profoundly at one with him.

God is very near us and utterly other, distant from us.

In meditation we see that the divine nearness is not so different, not necessarily even more comforting, than the distance.

As we meditate we come to understand that it is precisely God's distance from us that is our invitation to journey beyond ourselves.

God's nearness encourages us to keep journeying. But God's distance reminds us that we must never try to capture or to control God, because we can't.

The human journey is the invitation to expand into God's boundlessness.

By a strange paradox, as we journey into the infinite space of God's being we come closer to one another. True communion depends on people plumbing the depths of their own being, knowing themselves, and then revealing themselves known.

Love is fulfilled in the revealing of our true self to another who is equally real.

On the journey of meditation we say our mantra and let go of thoughts, plans, ideas and imaginings. So we learn the value of renunciation, of non-possessiveness.

We let go of our images of self. We let go of our desires. We let go of our fears and eventually even of our self-consciousness.

Renunciation enables us to enter communion with the other, and with all others, at a deep level of personal reality.

The solitude of meditation is thus the foundation stone on which we build all relationships, leading to communion, true communion with ourselves, with others, and with God.

In the silence of our own heart we enter the harmony that reveals to us our oneness with all.

> Then put on the garments that suit God's chosen people, his own, his beloved: compassion, kindness, humility, gentleness, patience. Be forbearing with one another, and forgiving, where any of you has cause for complaint: you must forgive as the Lord forgave you. To crown all, there must be love, to bind all together and to complete the whole. Let Christ's peace be arbiter in your hearts; to this peace you were called as members of a single body.
>
> *Colossians 3.12–15*

# *Truth*

To learn to meditate we have to be prepared to enter into the whole truth, and that's the challenge of it: the truth about ourselves, the truth about others, and the ultimate truth of all reality.

To meditate it's necessary to learn that our meditation is unconditional. Our commitment is to the whole truth. It would be a mistake to start meditating unless we were ready to begin to launch out into this readiness to face the truth.

For so much of life we keep all kinds of filters in place, in order to filter the coming-in and going-out of truth. These filters are necessary only so long as we live on the surface, trying, with much energy, to protect or project our self-image.

But in meditating we commit ourselves to living not at the surface level of self-image, or at the shallow level of half-reality, but to reality as it is.

We do this by a steady, daily process. That's why it is so important to meditate every day. It is a steady process of redirecting all our energy from defensive and protective channels into creativity.

This leads us beyond protecting our image of ourselves and instead to set out on the road to self-discovery. Each of us is invited to discover the heart of the mystery of life itself.

There is only one ultimate human tragedy: not to live to the full the gift of life that is given to us. In meditating we seek to respond to that gift of life at the very depth of our own being.

Why do we build these protective defences around ourselves? Because we are not sure whether other people will accept us as we are. And probably the reason for this uncertainty is that we do not really accept ourselves as we are. Our fears about ourselves must be dissolved.

Meditation is a redirection of our energy beyond ourselves to ultimate reality, to God, to the certainty of being accepted.

Meditation is putting ourselves in touch with the source of the energy of all creation. This means that we abandon our self-protectiveness, the self-assertiveness born of insecurity, our self-obsession, and we enter the reality of God.

The marvel of the Christian revelation is that God is love, and experiencing that personally is what our meditation is about.

Getting in touch with love as the basic energy of creation that is flowing in the depths of our heart, our own being, is finding the energy who is God, who is love.

This is an astonishing, life-changing experience, leading to a complete transformation of perception. In the heart of each one of us is found the source of endless infinite love.

This is the love that casts out all our fear. By casting out fear love enables us to become truly ourselves, to be the person we are called to be. To abandon all our images and all our defences.

Becoming ourselves means simply to put ourselves in full contact with this power, this energy we call love.

The reality of God's Spirit dwelling within us does not depend on our thinking about it. Indeed, it becomes a personal reality for us when we stop thinking about it and instead enter into the loving awareness of it in silence.

This is why in meditation we do not think about ourselves or think about God or think about anything. Meditation is an experience of personal communion in the depths of our being.

We each have the capacity to do this if only we learn to develop it. To be *with*. To be with ourselves, wholly present to ourselves. To be with others, wholly present to them.

This being with self and others develops the capacity to be wholly present to God. Our existence is the personal invitation to discover this reality of being for ourselves. The way of discovery is to enter profound silence and to remain in that silence in humble fidelity.

We must understand how simple meditating is. First, simply sit still. Each of us has to learn to do that. It's the first step away from egoism. Away from self-obsession. Then, sit as upright as you can. Be alert.

Then, closing your eyes gently, begin to repeat your word, your mantra. The word I recommend you to repeat is the Aramaic prayer-word '*Maranatha*' as four equally stressed syllables: Ma-ra-na-tha.

The art of meditating is learning to recite and repeat your mantra, very gently, and very faithfully. By practice each of us learns how to say the mantra from the beginning to the end of our meditation.

We all find when we begin that the mind wanders. Sometimes it careers off for long periods. The art is to come gently back to the saying of the mantra as soon as we realize this has happened again.

So, to learn to meditate we need to learn to be patient with ourselves as we learn to be faithful to the daily times of meditation. It is all learning, all the way.

The minimum time I suggest for a period of meditation is 20 minutes. It takes about that just to let the mind begin to settle into clarity and stillness. Put 20 minutes aside every morning and every evening.

Don't succumb to the temptation of just floating. You may find, after saying the mantra even for a few moments, that you become very calm. The temptation then is just to possess the peace.

Learning to meditate is learning to be in a state of complete non-possessiveness. Don't succumb to the temptation of holding on to an interesting thought or insight. Let it go. Don't become attached to a feeling of peace or bliss. Let it go.

When we meditate, either alone or together, we must learn to be as still as possible, and as silent as possible.

There is a great deal we can do for each other by this commitment to silence in our commitment to the discipline of meditation. Remember, the basic energy of the universe is love.

Essentially, we are learning to love by meditating like this. To be loved. To be love to all we know and meet. Love enters the world of human relationships through us in this way.

Love strengthens every one of us, heals every one of us. It brings all of us together into the fullest human response to the gift of our own creation through the Spirit of the God who is love:

If you love me you will obey my commands; and I will ask the Father, and he will give you another to be your Advocate, who will be with you for ever – the Spirit of truth. The world cannot receive him, because the world neither sees nor knows him; but you know him, because he dwells with you and is in you.

*John 14.15–17*

# Time and Reality

L ove teaches us about the relationship between time and eternity.

The experience of prayer is an entry into the eternity of God – in the now.

In meditation we become alive *now* with the life of Christ. We are enlivened with the life of Christ. We learn that what is eternal is not out of time but is fully present.

Past, present and future are drawn together in the centrality of the present moment of the now.

It is important to be clear in our perception of time and eternity. Meditation leads into the experience of being so deeply rooted in the present moment that we pierce the veil of time.

By being wholly at one with Christ in the present moment in prayer we transcend the limitations of our own separateness.

We know from our own experience of life that we find something very similar to this when we are at one with the person we love.

Transcending ourselves in that love we know ourselves anew in the larger context of another's love for us and of our love for another.

In prayer we go beyond our own limitations and enter the experience of Christ's love for us. This is his grace, his gift to us. This is what he desires to share with us.

He shares with us his own experience of his infinite love for the Father and the Father's infinite love for him.

It might sound arrogant to say we can experience this – or meta-physical fantasy. And it would be were it not for the invitation Christ extends to each of us to be alive and to have life in all its fullness.

The fullness of the life Christ offers us is eternal life, life without limitations. The mystery is that that fullness of life is offered to us now – in this life we are living now, not in future lives.

Learning to be alive fully shows us that there must be constant personal development. The invitation of life is to grow, develop and mature. One element of maturity is a growing capacity to be in the present moment more and more fully, more and more peacefully, more and more lovingly. That's why it is so important to meditate every day, faithfully, every morning and every evening. This is what we are learning.

Each time we meditate, each time we say our mantra, we are entering more fully into the process of deepening our capacity to be wholly in the now. By the daily practice we build our lives on the eternal rock that is Christ.

It's so easy for our lives to pass before our eyes in the way we look at the changing patterns of a kaleidoscope.

It's easy to live our short lives being tossed around by waves of fortune, never knowing where we will wash up next, or how long we will be there.

The challenge is to find the underlying constant pattern. It is to find the ground under our feet that does not give way in life's earthquakes, to find the rock who is Christ.

To find Christ in our hearts and then respond to our daily lives rooted in his *knowledge* that is love. To respond humbly with a power that we know comes from beyond us.

From this knowledge comes the ability to go beyond ourselves. The confidence that this knowledge gives us is not arrogance. It is, however, a humble sureness of touch that springs from our total dependence on God.

A dependence on God is not slavery or addiction but pure gift and perfect freedom.

And this is what we discover in meditation in the silence and in the gradual deepening of it.

We discover our total dependence on God and that discovery brings us to humility.

It also brings us to great joy because we realize that the dependence is a dependency of love. His invitation is to be one with him, to be one with the Father. That is the gift of Christ to us that unites time and eternity.

St Paul, writing to the Corinthians, describes this experience:

> No wonder we do not lose heart! Though our outward humanity is in decay, yet day by day we are inwardly renewed. Our troubles are slight and short-lived; and their outcome an eternal glory which outweighs them far. Meanwhile our eyes are fixed, not on the things that are seen, but on the things that are unseen: for what is seen passes away; what is unseen is eternal. For we know that if the earthly frame that houses us today should be demolished, we possess a building which God has provided – a house not made by human hands, eternal, and in heaven.

> *2 Corinthians 4.16–18—5.1*

All of us are invited today, now, to live out of that eternal power. An eternal power that is present always in our hearts.

All we need do is to attend to it with every fibre of our being.

# Levels of Distraction

The purpose of meditation is to learn to live our lives as fully as possible in the presence of God.

Learning to live in this presence means being energized with God's energy. We know from the gospel that this energy is love.

Learning to meditate is learning how to remain constantly in this presence and constantly to be renewed by it.

To learn anything we have first to learn to pay attention, to listen. We have to learn the humility to listen and then to begin the simple tasks we are being taught. If you want to learn a musical instrument you have to learn to play the scales. If you want to learn a language, you have to learn the elementary grammar. And you have to be content to learn that because without the foundation of that simple knowledge no progress is possible.

In learning to meditate the first thing to learn is to sit well with a good posture. The essential rule of posture is that the spine be upright and the essential rule of sitting is that we sit still. Elementary and simple – but not easy at first!

We learn physical stillness not to get the body out of the way but so that body and spirit can both be harmoniously involved and unified in our meditation. Meditation is a complete unity of body, mind and spirit – still and present to God.

We have to prepare ourselves to meditate. The first preparation is the goodness we practise in everyday living. It is of great importance that we learn to prepare ourselves by simple kindness, forgiveness, simple goodness.

Then the immediate preparation is the quiet of the place we choose to meditate. Then quietness of body prepares us for the inner stillness of the Spirit that opens us to total attentiveness of body and spirit.

So at each meditation period take a little time to find a comfortable sitting posture. Close your eyes, and gently and silently, in your heart, begin to say your mantra. If you say 'Maranatha' say it as four equally stressed syllables: Ma-ra-na-tha. If you can do so comfortably breathe the whole word in and then breathe out in silence. If you can't, then breathe in Ma-ra and breathe out na-tha.

That's all you have to do for the entire time of your meditation. Say your word from beginning to end.

Meditation is like a mining operation. We go down deep, mining into our hearts. In the Christian vision this descent into the depths of our being is to uncover the great treasure that each one of us possesses, the Spirit of God in the field of our heart.

It's useful, if you can, to meditate early in the morning and in the early evening. But everyone has to find in the circumstances of their life the times that suit them best.

But if you can, meditate first thing in the morning and in the early evening, before eating. It's good to come to your meditation purified. You could wash at least your face and hands, to be purified of the dust of the day or the drowsiness of the night. This prepares the body to be alert for the purity of meditation.

Then we prepare our spirit by regular, calm, deep breathing. All this just sets the scene for the serious work we are entering into.

Meditation is entering into the presence of the One who is. It's in the presence of the One who is that each person learns to be. To hear the call to be the person we are called to be.

To listen this deeply and purely we must pass beyond all images, above all the image we have of ourselves.

So when we begin to meditate we divest ourselves of all masks. We set them down on the ground beside us and begin to become the real person we are in absolute simplicity.

We are saying our mantra not to impress anyone, nor to create any further image of ourselves – a spiritual image of ourselves as meditators, for example. Rather, we say it in order to leave all images, thoughts and words behind, in the 'cloud of forgetting'; so we can be still in utter simplicity.

Learn to live with distractions. There are different levels of distraction. There is the distraction that comes from the streaming immediacy of our lives: the last TV programme we were watching, the news or advertising, the conversation we were just having, the problems we were just solving. We let all that go as we listen to the mantra.

There are more personal distractions, such as the problems of relationships with family or friends, problems in our work or career, the loneliness we sometimes suffer. All these, too, we must let go, by saying the mantra, as we come into the presence of the One who is, who is love.

Then there are spiritual distractions, wondering about our spiritual progress, comparing our experience to someone else's, analysing the kind of consciousness we are in. We must let go of all these distractions.

We let go of them all by being faithful to the mantra. So, if you find you are thinking about a soap opera or a family problem or about your spiritual progress, drop it immediately and return to the mantra: Ma-ra-na-tha.

The greatest of all distractions is self-consciousness. This is the root of distraction; it arises because of the innate tendency we all have to look at ourselves. By meditating we look beyond ourselves to God; not at God but into God.

So the mantra expands our awareness way beyond ourselves.

The first levels of distraction are external, stimulated by reference points 'outside' us. Self-consciousness is internal. And the power of meditation is that it tackles the source of all distraction at root. The root is ego, self-consciousness.

In meditating we learn to stop thinking about ourselves, and instead to go on a journey looking ahead in faith, with love and trust. And staying on the journey.

The test and guarantee we are staying on the journey is that we say our mantra and constantly return to it.

This is as Jesus describes it in the Gospel of Matthew, finding the treasure within:

> The kingdom of Heaven is like treasure lying buried in a field. The man who found it, buried it again; and for sheer joy went and sold everything he had, and bought that field. Here is another picture of the kingdom of Heaven. A merchant looking out for fine pearls found one of very special value; so he went and sold everything he had, and bought it.
>
> *Matthew 13.44–46*

Saying the mantra is just like that: letting go of everything and resting in God.

# The Ordinary Shot through
# with the Extraordinary

.    May he strengthen you, in his glorious might, with ample
power to meet whatever comes with fortitude, patience, and
joy; and to give thanks to the Father who has made you fit to
share the heritage of God's people in the realm of light.

*Colossians 1.11–12*

St Paul invites us to be strengthened with divine strength and
with God's power that is always more than enough. We must
remember that this faith-conviction is what Christianity is all
about.

The Christian life is learning to live out of this ample power of
God, not looking at our lives just in terms of how we can cope by
ourselves, but realizing that there is an unlimited source of power
reaching to us; thus the call to 'share the heritage of God's people
in the realm of light'.

This is the most extraordinary language describing an extraordinary experience. The glorious might and ample power of God

59

are offered to each one of us to enable us to meet whatever comes with fortitude – that is, with hope and courage and patience.

This divine energy develops the human capacity to stay with what must be gone through. It also releases the joy to expand our hearts and celebrate what must be celebrated.

For the Christian, living in touch with this power of God, there must be a coherence between the ordinary and the extraordinary.

The invitation that Jesus gives us is to see that the ordinary fabric of our lives, the simple things of every day, are interwoven with transcendence, the divine goodness, divine power and divine love.

The vision that Jesus proposes is a practical way of living day to day so that the human and the divine are brought into a wholly harmonious union. Jesus himself is the living witness of this harmony.

The Incarnation is the revelation of the human potential for union with God. In Jesus we see this union perfectly realized.

We may need to remind ourselves that Jesus' ordinary life at Nazareth is of no less importance to us than his public ministry, Passion, Death and Resurrection. Catholic piety has always understood this in the popular devotions to the Holy Family, to Mary the mother and homemaker, to Joseph the carpenter, to the child Jesus.

Anyone committed to the pilgrimage of meditation needs to remember the utter ordinariness of meditation, the ordinariness of the daily return to the practice every morning and every evening, in simplicity of spirit.

Sitting down to meditate, without demands or expectations of extraordinary phenomena. Simply sitting to meditate because we know that is what our spirit requires. It's this ordinariness that gives meditation its potential for radical expansion of spirit beyond our separate selves into God.

The commitment to the simplicity of the practice is supremely important. When we sit down to meditate we leave behind all our analyses, all our thinking, and we are content to be in the presence.

If we want to live our lives to the full, then we must find our way into this perfect equilibrium of the human and the divine. And not just in theory. Our full humanity must be brought into this harmonious oneness with God.

The inspiring insight of the Christian vision is that this coherence is found in the person of Jesus. The mystery of the insight is that the experience of oneness, wholeness and harmony is found deep within ourselves.

It is found in the Spirit of God who dwells in our hearts. Meditation is the outward expression of our inward commitment to know and to be known by the presence of dwelling in our hearts.

Once we begin to move towards this reality, we start to understand that the ordinary is shot through with the extraordinary. We learn that we can no longer set the divine over against or only outside the human.

The Incarnation means that the coming of Jesus has changed the basic orientation of the human condition. The human person now has the capacity to respond fully to the 'glorious might' and 'ample power' of God through the Spirit of Jesus.

It is this power to respond that gives us the capacity to be definitively inserted into the realm of light; the capacity to be in God, to be unified, to be enlightened and to be utterly free within the unlimited, the infinite freedom of God.

The extraordinary thing is that the way to be open fully to this destiny is a way of such simplicity. The way of the one little word. A way that enables us to be humble, to be poor, and to be faithful.

As the New Testament shows us, the wonder of what we move into through this union with the spirit of Jesus is boundless:

> May he strengthen you, in his glorious might, with ample power to meet whatever comes with fortitude, patience, and joy; and to give thanks to the Father who has made you fit to share the heritage of God's people in the realm of light. He rescued us from the domain of darkness and brought us away into the kingdom of his dear Son, in whom our release is secured and our sins forgiven. He is the image of the invisible God; his is the primacy over all created things.
>
> *Colossians 1.11–15*

# Liberty of Spirit

Jesus says to humanity:

The truth will set you free.

*John 8.32*

Meditation is a way to perfect liberty of spirit. The call to this freedom is something that each of us has to respond fully to. It is the gift of our creation.

In meditation we respond to the depths of our own being so that we may attain this perfect liberty of spirit.

Especially when we are beginning to meditate we must understand it as a discipline. There is no liberty without discipline. Beginning to meditate is a commitment to that essential discipline of freedom.

Meditation is nothing whatsoever to do with magical technique. It involves the fullest human response through a daily discipline of love. Because it is practised daily it is also a lifetime discipline that leads us into an ever deeper liberty of spirit and celebration of life.

What is meditation? Silence, stillness, simplicity. In practical terms, it's simply learning to say our word, our mantra. The problem for most of us is that this way is so simple that we cannot believe it. We cannot really trust it and so we're constantly running to books and to commentaries on books.

We're trying to learn from other people's experience whereas it is our own experience that teaches us. This experience unfolds through the daily practice of learning to say our mantra and being content to say it.

The art is learning to say the mantra from the beginning to the end without interruption. It takes time and patience. You learn to let go of your ideas, to let go of the insights you have about yourself, or about God, or about meditation itself.

This is poverty of spirit. This way we learn what the first monastic teachers called the art of 'resting in the Lord'. The mantra is simply our way into that state of simple, trust-filled silence.

When you begin you are bound to have questions. 'Is this a complete waste of time?' 'Are these monks talking complete nonsense?' 'Are they talking through their hoods?' 'How long will it take?' 'Is there something quicker?'

The answer to all these questions is to continue to meditate. Ultimately it's the practice itself that is authenticating. It's not what I or any other teacher may say. It's the contact with your own spirit that authenticates your meditation.

The problem for us as men and women today is to be trusting enough, to be still enough, to be simple enough, just to be content to say our word. But when you doubt it remember these words of Jesus:

> Whoever does not accept the kingdom of God like a child will never enter it.

Mark 10.15

Jesus didn't say it would be easy, just simple. It *will* be hard at times, of course. But learning to say the mantra faithfully and humbly is our way into that childlike, simple trust and pure faith. In the tradition from which we speak the essential thing is the practice.

If you have just an hour a day to devote to your spiritual life, my recommendation is that you spend it in meditation as a half an hour in the morning and a half an hour in the evening. Don't waste as much as five minutes reading books on meditation. Enter into the experience yourself. I'm exaggerating but also I'm not. When you have really entered into the experience there will be time enough to read the books. We might even understand some of them at that stage! But even then the essential thing is the practice.

During these times we learn to be content to say our mantra. Forget all notions of progress. Forget about enlightenment. Forget about insight. Forget about yourself and say your mantra.

In this forgetting we will remember what liberty of spirit means.

I think we all know, deep down, that we have this call and capacity for liberty. We know that we cannot live our lives to the full if we are always trapped in trivia and distraction. If we are always absorbed in things that are passing away we are never free, never present.

Usually when we think of liberty we think of the freedom to do what we want. This freedom of choice is one important element in human life and dignity.

But the liberty of spirit which the New Testament speaks about is not just the freedom to *do*. It is above all the freedom, the true liberty, to *be*. To be who we are. To be one, with ourselves and others and with God. All our potentialities join together in a deep personal harmony at this degree of liberty.

The liberty of the New Testament is the ability to enter into our own personal and unique relationship with the One who is, with God. So, it's also the liberty to discover that this unique, personal relationship, to which each of us is summoned, *is* our relationship with all.

Through liberty we embrace our deepest capacity for relationship.

We are invited to discover our personal harmony and wholeness in our capacity for relationship. We must be sure we don't let the great invitation of life slip through our fingers by missing this invitation.

The unique gift of our creation is the potential to enter into harmony with the One and with all.

Of course we must be careful not to be intoxicated by these ideas about meditation or infatuated with the theory alone. Once we begin to encounter it in practice, in our own heart, the theory will fill us with wonder. But we must continue to encounter it personally.

That is why daily practice is of supreme importance. By it we learn to take our potentiality absolutely seriously, to understand that the Spirit of the One who created the universe dwells in our hearts and in silence is loving to all.

We have to enter our own heart to discover that Spirit within our own spirit.

# Open to the Moment of Love

St Paul wrote to the Romans:

> Have you forgotten that when we were baptized into union with Christ Jesus we were baptized into his death? By baptism we were buried with him, and lay dead, in order that, as Christ was raised from the dead in the splendour of the Father, so also we might set our feet upon the new path of life. For if we have become incorporate with him in a death like his, we shall also be one with him in a resurrection like his.
>
> *Romans 6.3–5*

To be a Christian is to be setting out on this 'new path of life'. We are able to do it because of the Resurrection of Christ, and because of his glory in which we are all invited to share.

What does this resurrection life mean?

From the New Testament it appears clearly that the risen Jesus could only be seen with the eyes of faith. On one occasion he was mistaken for a gardener, an ordinary workman, until he was suddenly recognized. All of us need clarified vision to see the risen Christ and all of life irradiated with his glory.

This vision happens in the new dimension of faith where we learn to see. To enter this vision of life we need the wisdom of this vision in order to penetrate beyond appearances.

We also need the sensitivity to open to a dimension of reality that is only revealed to those who can get into tune with the basic structure of reality. Those, that is, who understand from their own experience that the underpinning support of everything we see is the reality of God.

Meditation has always been understood as this way of vision. It has often been described as the process whereby we open the eyes of our heart and learn to see with love.

One of the best analogies for the process is falling in love. To everyone else the beloved still looks the same. But when we love someone deeply and unreservedly we see them in a quite new light. Their slightest gesture can convey a truth to us that no one else can see. Falling in love is such an important, profound experience for this awakening because it takes us beyond ourselves into the reality of the other, to hold and be held.

Profound meditation is of the same order. We abandon our isolated view of life and we learn in the silence and discipline of our daily meditation to travel beyond our own limitations into the limitless ocean of God's love.

By entering into silence, by opening the eye of our heart to the light of infinity, we begin to see with a new power of vision. We see with clarity, with a sharpness and acuity of vision that is startling, and with a profundity that is intoxicating.

What do we see? We see knowledge. We see the One who knows

that he is. We see oneness everywhere and we know that all divisions must be transcended. We see love.

What do we know? We know that all previous knowledge and wisdom is nothing compared to the supreme reality of the love who is. All is revealed in this love.

The revelation takes place in the moment of God's choosing. The only ultimate tragedy in life is not to be ready for this moment of love; not to be ready for this time of revelation in which time is transcended.

Our daily commitment to the discipline of meditation is our setting out on the road of faith (that's the vision too), preparing our hearts for the moment and leaving egoism behind and, with it, all division.

Discipline is the humble acknowledgement that all we can learn, all we can experience, is in the direct gift of God. When we meditate we are simply acknowledging that God is God. God is One and God is love.

Each of us is summoned into the oneness of that love. Our meditation is our way to that oneness, our way to that resurrection, our way to that 'path of new life'.

# Learning to Expect Nothing

We all start meditation – more or less – from scratch. The difficulty is putting aside our previous notions about the spiritual path or contemplation.

When we begin we are likely to come to meditation with all sorts of expectations: it's going to bring us peace and enlightenment; it's going to help us concentrate better; it's going to help us in our personal relationships.

Once there was a programme on television during which six regular meditators of our Community were interviewed. The interviewer kept asking, 'Well, why do you keep meditating?' Their replies didn't satisfy his expectations. Basically they all replied that it seemed to be the thing to do. So he asked, 'Well, what happens?'

I could understand his question. Yet what we have to understand about meditation is that we are not doing it to make something happen. We are not meditating in order to get some special insight we can describe to an interviewer, or to our ego.

In fact we are not meditating to gain any possession whatsoever.

Quite the reverse. We meditate so that we can *dispossess* ourselves – not just of ideas and insights but also of our very selves.

The essential motivation of Christian meditation is that we become absorbed in God where we lose all sense of ourselves and find ourselves only in God.

St Catherine of Genoa, one of the great women mystics, wrote: 'I know myself only in God.' That's a difficult concept to come to terms with or to explain on television because we are trained to be such materialists, even in things of the spirit.

We are brought up to be such controllers, such possessors, such collectors. To sit down and to voluntarily make ourselves poor, to dispossess ourselves as we enter into the presence of God, is the greatest challenge there could be.

Sitting still helps to meet this challenge. We instinctively want to run, to grab, to move. Stillness is of great importance when we meditate so try to sit as still as you can. Don't move your limbs. If your ear begins to itch and you want to scratch it, ignore it. Just sit still. That's the very important first step away from the egoism of acquisition that we have to leave behind in meditation, by reciting the mantra at ever deeper levels of silence.

'And what happens?' the interviewer, the ego, asks. Basically it doesn't matter what happens. All that matters is to say your mantra and to continue saying it for the entire time of the meditation.

It's the experience of most meditators, particularly beginners, that the half-hours you spend meditating in the morning and in the evening will often seem a complete and utter waste of time.

You get up from your meditation and say, 'Now, what did I get out of that?' Nothing. What happened? Nothing. Wonderful! This is when meditating is an act of purest faith.

When we sit to meditate we put ourselves in touch with a great and glorious tradition of men and women who throughout the ages have understood that *the* greatest wisdom is to leave self behind. In their own experience they understood the words of Jesus:

> Anyone who wishes to be a follower of mine must leave self behind.
>
> *Mark 8.34*

They set out on this path to absolute liberty of spirit and found it to be the path on which we leave behind all our limitations and enter the infinite generosity of God's love.

A couple of years ago a man came regularly to our introductory meditation group and every week, each Monday evening, he would ask the same question: 'How long have I got to keep this up for? I've been meditating now for three (four, five, six) months. I've been faithful to it every morning and evening.' Then he paused, looking forlorn, and said, 'Absolutely nothing is happening.' He was getting irritated with me too, I think. He added, 'It's all very well for you to sit there and say that I've got to have no expectations, that I've just got to accept the discipline of it, but surely to God something is going to happen one day?'

That went on for weeks until one evening he wasn't there. But as everyone was leaving after the session had ended, he arrived. I could see that something had happened to him. There was a big smile all over his face. 'You know, an extraordinary thing has just happened,' he said. 'As I was turning the corner at the bottom of the hill to come up here a young kid pushed his bike in front of my car. I could see he did it deliberately. I swerved and my car just tapped it and I stopped. Immediately three kids surrounded the car and said, "Come on, you've got to pay me compensation, you've wrecked my bike." I was amazed how calm I was. I'm not normally calm in situations like that. I just said "OK. Let's get the bike into the car and you get in too, and we'll drive round to the police station." '

The crisis dissolved and the kids ran off. But, throughout the whole incident he was aware of his calmness and the controlling attitude towards what was happening. Then he said to me, 'I don't suppose anything is ever going to happen in my meditation, but I do see that it's going to change my life. In fact, it's already started to.'

That's true for all of us who meditate. It manifests differently according to where we are coming from, and what corners we are turning in life.

What's the great test of whether your meditation is working and you are making progress? I don't advise you to rate yourself, but the great test is 'Are you growing in love? Are you growing in patience? Are you growing in understanding and compassion?'

That is the effect of meditation. For some of us it takes longer. With some the end of egoism requires a big struggle. Often we are carried more or less kicking and screaming into the Kingdom of heaven.

The important thing is not to bother how long it takes. It doesn't matter, as long as you are truly on the way.

The thing I wish I could communicate to every one of you is that we are on a journey. The journey is away from self; away from egoism; away from selfishness; away from isolation. It's a way into the infinite love of God.

The fidelity to the path simplifies us. Jesus says to leave self behind, to let go of all our possessions in order to follow him into this kingdom of selflessness. But he also says,

> Whoever does not enter the kingdom of God like a child will never enter it.
>
> *Mark 10.15*

Saying the mantra each morning and evening is just this entry into a childlike state where we place our full confidence and trust in God.

Whatever gift God gives we receive with simplicity and joy. Whatever barrenness God leads us through we accept it with the same simplicity and fundamental joy.

The greatest joy is to enter this oneness in which all desire leaves us. A oneness that brings us into complete harmony, a harmony with our own spirit. A harmony with the Spirit of God, harmony with all creation.

The only quality we require for this journey is re-committing ourselves to the pilgrimage. Where we are, as we are, now.

Don't bother about distraction. Don't bother if you give up meditating for a day or a year. Start again. Don't bother if you miss your meditation one morning or evening. Try not to miss it the next day. Keep returning. Of supreme importance is that we are on the pilgrimage and that we stay on the pilgrimage.

Be encouraged by St Paul writing to the Corinthians:

> For the love of Christ leaves us no choice, when once we have reached the conclusion that one man died for all and therefore all mankind has died. His purpose in dying for all was that men, while still in life, should cease to live for themselves, and should live for him who for their sake died and was raised to life.

> *2 Corinthians 5.14–15*

We have what we need to finish the journey. Every meditation is dying to self and rising to new life in Christ.

# Everything that Is One

We tend to think of reality in compartments. We study politics, economics, physics, metaphysics, theology and all the subjects seem to stand self-sufficient in their own little categories. Of course, if any of us were to be challenged on this we would say that these divisions are only for the purpose of study and all reality is, in fact, one.

But do we really believe that? Do we know that? Do we understand it for ourselves? What, for example, do we think of the gulf between the finite and the infinite? What do we think of the gulf between the mortal and the immortal? Do we really believe that 'all that is is one'?

It's my feeling that one of the major causes of the state of anxiety prevailing among our contemporaries is that they do not believe in such oneness. And so there seems to them to be an infinite gap between the mortal and the immortal, between dream and reality.

I believe meditation is so important for all of us today because it teaches us, right in our own hearts, right in the centre of our consciousness where we can understand it, that indeed God is all in all. All compartments, all divisions, are illusory.

We must learn that all life is energy. The smallest plant, the most complex movement of the brain – both are alive and their life consists in the vitalizing energy that keeps them living and evolving and drives them to communicate their own energy to other forms of life, to expansion of life.

So I think each of us who is alive is invited by that energy of aliveness, as mature people, to come into contact with and personally to know the mystery of God in our own hearts.

The mystery of God is the mystery of the divine energy of life. Each of us must learn from our own experience that the source of this energy encountered within our deepest self is limitless, infinite, self-communicating love.

We must know that God is the ground of our being. God is the ground of all being. Once we begin to make contact with this reality in the depths of our own heart we are led into the understanding of the most profound and yet most simple truth: that there is an ontological continuity in all being. All is one.

We are all one in God. And that is why we must love one another and be open to one another's love.

Everything we see and everything we cannot see is a form of energy. Anything that is perceptible as a form is an expression of something else, something deeper. All form is an expression of God who is the formless energy of all being. So everything reveals his wonder.

The wonder of life is that these forms of energy, which we call reality, do not comprise a static hierarchy. All creation is in a state of flowing back into its source. This is why mortality, which is only a changing of form, is the mark of creation. Through this principle of mortality everything is being transformed from one form to another.

St Paul put it like this: 'Though our outward humanity is in decay, yet day by day we are inwardly renewed . . . Our troubles are slight . . . their outcome an eternal glory . . .' (2 Corinthians 4.16–17)

At the level of biological life, too, we have our share in the divine flow of energy, in all its variety, in all its complex simplicity. The wonder of the Christian understanding of the world is that this creative flux of energy, through all these different forms of matter and spirit have a guiding principle, and this focal point is their goal.

The guiding principle, the direction of this cosmic flow, its purposefulness, is the Spirit. The Spirit, which is beyond form, and yet which informs all form.

The focal point, on which everything in creation is aligned, is the Logos, the Word, the Son. The marvel of the Christian vocation is to understand that in the Word made flesh we ourselves are focused and clarified.

And the end, the goal of all, the goal of this whole flow of energy is the Father who is the unknown knower, the source of all.

When we sit down to meditate, every morning and every evening, we can do so in utter humility at the sheer marvel and the wonder of our human calling. We must sit in absolute confidence that in the person of Jesus we find the key to it all, real continuity between the finite and the infinite, between the mortal and the immortal. Love turns the key because Jesus lives in our hearts.

If we see this for ourselves through our meditation we will not read words like these of St Paul as triumphalism, but as a cry of universal wonder and delight:

> But the truth is, Christ was raised to life – the firstfruits of the harvest of the dead. For since it was a man who brought death into the world, a man also brought resurrection of the dead. As in Adam all men die, so in Christ all will be brought to life; but each in his own proper place: Christ the firstfruits, and after-wards, at his coming, those who belong to Christ. Then comes the end, when he delivers up the kingdom to God the Father, after abolishing every kind of domination, authority, and power. For he is destined to reign until God has put all enemies under his feet; and the last enemy to be abolished is death. Scripture says, 'He has put all things in subjection under his feet.' But in saying 'all things', it clearly means to exclude God who subordinates them; and when all things are thus subject to him, then the Son himself will also be made subordi-nate to God who made all things subject to him, and thus God will be all in all.
>
> *1 Corinthians 15.20–28*

Our human meaning and our Christian calling is to enter into that oneness now. We must begin now. The Kingdom is simply the experience when God is all in all.

# *Being Present Now*

To understand what this oneness I am speaking of really means you have to appreciate that the essence of meditation is not thinking but presence.

We learn to be wholly present in the moment that we are now. So much of our time we spend thinking what we will do in the future or about what we have done in the past. Most of the time our minds are wholly distracted with memories, daydreams and plans.

By meditating we can learn to become wholly inserted into the now of the present moment. We learn this in the tradition I have been describing by saying our word, our meditation word, our mantra, with pure attention.

Learn to say the mantra from the beginning of your meditation until the end by returning to it whenever you are distracted and slip out of the present into past, future or fantasy.

Whatever thoughts come to you, however brilliant, whatever idea, however original, let them go. Don't hang on to anything but listen to the sound of your mantra. This leads to an open attention, a deep attention of spirit. It is a mindfulness of what is not what has been or not what might be but what *is*. The first step, and in a sense the only step, is, therefore, mindfulness, attention.

The second step is the second degree of the first step, but it is more like a leap or a plunge into the very basis of all that is. The second step is the realization that God is. That God is present. That God is now and, perhaps most wonderful of all, that God is mindful of all.

People often wonder when they start to meditate about the apparent gap between their faith in God and their faithful recitation of the mantra.

It can seem when we begin that because we are told to leave all thoughts, words and images behind in our meditation that we must leave God behind too. When we are meditating we are thinking of God. If we are truly attentive to the mantra we *cannot* image God. We *cannot* construct any idea or ikon of God.

In the context of this pure attention, pure faith, we learn that all images, ideas, memories and words fall short of the reality we are paying attention to. They are unreal. They are illusion. So in meditation we realize that God is not an absent memory or an abstract dream. God is.

In the simplicity and faithfulness of the practice God is known not only as a reality we think about or imagine or talk to or analyse, but also as all reality. To go forward to meet God in pure attention is to know and to be known by God.

To know is to love. To be loved is to be known. To be loved by

God is to love God. We need to divest ourselves of all the intermediary processes. All images, thoughts and language must go.

The simplifying practice of saying the mantra teaches us to pay full attention to what is *directly*. To pay full attention to the One who is *personally*. To prepare for this we learn the discipline of mindfulness.

We learn the discipline of selflessness, not to be thinking of ourselves. Not to be caught up in a web of our own self-reflective weaving. Not to be snared by external circumstances. But to live from the depth of our own being, from the depth of being itself.

Meditation is a discipline of presence. By stillness of body and spirit we learn to be wholly present to ourselves, to our situation, to our place. It is not running away. By staying rooted in our own being we become present to its source. We become rooted in being itself. Through all the changing circumstances of life nothing can shake us.

The process is gradual. It requires patience. And faithfulness. And discipline. And humility.

The humility of meditation is to put aside all self-important questioning. To put aside self-importance means to experience ourselves poor, divested of ego, as we learn how to be. To be present to the presence. We learn, not out of our own cleverness, but from the source of wisdom itself, the Spirit of God.

When you begin practice is most important. To learn to meditate you must meditate every day. None of us can really follow this path, regardless of how long or how short a time we've been on it, without the daily commitment, a daily fidelity. This means we come to love the path.

When you find you are straying from the mantra, or from the daily practice, return to it. Be patient with yourself. It will take time, patience and love. Don't meditate for results. The only sufficient motive for meditating is that God is.

These words from the prophet Isaiah say it:

> I was there to be sought by a people who did not ask, to be found by men who did not seek me.

*Isaiah 65.1*

# *Hope*

St Paul wrote to the Romans:

> Therefore, now that we have been justified through faith, let us continue at peace with God through our Lord Jesus Christ, through whom we have been allowed to enter the sphere of God's grace, where we now stand. Let us exult in the hope of the divine splendour that is to be ours. More than this: let us even exult in our present sufferings, because we know that suffering trains us to endure, and endurance brings proof that we have stood the test, and this proof is the ground of hope. Such a hope is no mockery, because God's love has flooded our inmost heart through the Holy Spirit he has given us.
>
> *Romans 5.1–5*

If you have been meditating long enough you know from your own experience that practice teaches us to meditate without expectations. We learn that the road we are treading is the way of dispossession. We even let go of our desire for wisdom, for knowledge, for holiness, for God.

Once we enter the experience of pure prayer in meditation we understand the limitation of praying for things, for passing concerns. We know of course that these are known to God. We *can* 'pray for' them if we wish. But increasingly we are over-whelmed by the sheer wonder of the experience of prayer itself; the wonder of entering into the limitlessness of Christ's prayer, of entering the uncharted, unchartable seas of the divine reality, to describe which there are no words.

We may also see that praying for things is often merely strengthening and indulging our own desires. We must be very clear about this, however painful to see.

But to pass beyond all desire is not to pass beyond hope.

Christian hope is at the very heart of our commitment to the practice of meditation. It's useful to understand the difference between hopes and hope.

Hopes are always limited. We hope for this or that. But hope itself is the realization of the infinite and so to enter into full Christian hope we must abandon all hopes. These are our desires.

Desires are everything that comes under the heading of wanting.

Hope is a kind of bliss. It is the bliss arising from the supreme confidence that fills the experience of prayer. Our potential is at once realized and extended.

Hope arises from knowing that there *is* a way, a sure way. Maybe a hard way, maybe demanding, but certain. Hope arises from knowing that we *are* on the way. Maybe we have only taken the first feeble, faltering steps. Maybe we still carry old baggage and are impeded by all our old inconstancy. All our stupidity.

Nevertheless we are on the way. Knowing this is the source of the bliss that is hope.

The hope growing in our heart is the certainty that Christ is the way. He is the way to eternal life, limitless life; life without beginning or end.

The way we are on takes us to a life that is always in a state of expansion. The knowledge we discover in the silence is that he who is true is the way.

This is not something that can be discovered in any book, or any lecture or any discussion. It is only to be discovered in silence; the poverty and humility of silence.

The challenge of the daily meditation is to enter, every day, more deeply into that silence. In the silence we will learn everything that is needed. Hope is this supreme confidence. There is bliss in that hope because, as St Paul says, it:

> is no mockery . . . because God's love has flooded our inmost heart . . .

> *Romans 5.5*

The paradox is that we must transcend our hopes so that we may arrive at hope itself. Hope *is* bliss. It is entry into divinization.

The extraordinary hope in the Christian vision is that each one of us is invited to enter into the self-transcendence that is in God. This means to enter and to share in, to become part of, God's limitless freedom, God's limitless love.

All we have to learn is to be silent. To put our desires aside. To put the impulse to possess aside. And to learn the faithfulness of the daily practice.

# Bibliography and
# Recorded Talks

## Books

*Awakening*, London, Arthur James Ltd, 1997

*Christian Meditation: The Gethsemani Talks*, The World Community for Christian Meditation 1977; Medio Media, 1999

*Community of Love*, London, Darton, Longman & Todd, 1990; New York, Continuum, 1999

*John Main: A Biography in Text and Photos*, ed. Paul Harris, Medio Media, 2001

*John Main: Essential Writings*, ed. Laurence Freeman OSB, Mary-Knoll, NY, Orbis Books, 2002

*Letters from the Heart: Christian Monasticism and the Renewal of Community*, New York, Crossroad, 1982

*Moment of Christ: The Path of Meditation*, London, Darton, Longman & Todd, 1984; New York, Crossroad, 1984

*The Joy of Being: Daily Readings*, London, Darton, Longman & Todd, 1987; USA, Templegate

*The Heart of Creation: The Meditative Way*, London, Darton, Longman & Todd, 1988; New York, Crossroad, 1988

*The Inner Christ*, London, Darton, Longman & Todd, 1987 (combines *Word into Silence, Moment of Christ* and *The Present Christ*)

*Silence and Stillness in Every Season: Daily Readings with John Main*, Paul Harris, Darton, Longman & Todd, 1997

*The Present Christ: Further Steps in Meditation*, London, Darton, Longman & Todd, 1985; New York, Crossroad, 1985

*The Way of Unknowing: Expanding Spiritual Horizons through Meditation*, London, Darton, Longman & Todd, 1989; New York, Crossroad, 1989

*Word into Silence*, London, Darton, Longman & Todd, 1980; New York, Paulist Press, 1981

*Word Made Flesh*, ed. Laurence Freeman OSB, London, Darton, Longman & Todd, 1993; New York, Continuum, 1998

## CDs/cassette tapes

*The Life and Teachings of John Main*, ed. Laurence Freeman OSB, Medio Media, 2002

*Being on the Way*, Medio Media, 1991

*Christian Meditation: The Essential Teaching*, Medio Media, 1991

*Communitas*, Volumes 1–5, Medio Media, 1991

*Fully Alive*, Medio Media, 1991

*In the Beginning*, Medio Media, 1991

*The Christian Mysteries*, Medio Media, 1979

*The Door to Silence*, Medio Media, 1985

*The Last Conferences*, Medio Media, 1991

*Word Made Flesh*, Medio Media, 1991

# *About the World Community for Christian Meditation*

The World Community for Christian Meditation took form in 1991. It continues John Main's legacy in teaching Christian meditation and his work of restoring the contemplation dimension of Christian faith in the life of the Church.

The Community is now directed by Laurence Freeman OSB, a student of John Main and a Benedictine monk of the Olivetan Congregation. The World Community has its International Centre and a retreat centre in London. There are a number of centres in other parts of the world. The Community is thus a 'monastery without walls', a family of national communities and emerging communities in over 100 countries. The foundation of this Community is the local meditation group, which meets weekly in homes, parishes, offices, hospitals, prisons and colleges. The World Community works closely with many Christian churches.

Annually it runs the John Main Seminar and The Way of Peace. It also sponsors retreats, schools for the training of teachers of meditation seminars, lectures and other programmes. It contributes to interfaith dialogues, and in recent years particularly with Buddhists and Muslims. A quarterly spiritual letter with news of the Community is mailed and also available online. Weekly readings can be sent direct by email. Information on current programmes, connections to national co-ordinators and the location of meditation groups can be found on the Community website, www.wccm.org, which also offers a range of online audio talks. This site is the hub of a growing internet family: the websites of national communities and special interests such as the teaching of meditation to children and the contemporary spirituality of priests.

Medio Media is the communication and publishing arm of the Community and offers a wide range of books, audio and videos to support the practice of meditation. The online bookstore is at www.mediomedia.org.

## Contact Details

### The International Centre
The World Community of Christian Meditation
St Mark's, Myddelton Square
London EC1R 1XX
Tel: 44 20 7278 2070
Fax: 4 20 7713 6346
Email: mail@wccm.org
www.wccm.org

### Australia
Australian Christian Meditation Community
PO Box 246
Uralla
New South Wales 2358
Australia
Tel: 61 2 9904 4638
Email: palmy@ozemail.com
www.christianmeditationaustralia.org

### Belgium
Christelijk Meditatie Centrum
Beiaardlaan 1
B-1850 Grimbergen
Belgium
Tel/Fax: 32 2 305 7513
Email:ccm@pandora.be
www.christmed.be

**Brazil**
Comunidade de Meditação Cristã
Caixa postal 62559
CEP 22252 Rio de Janeiro
Brazil
Tel: +55 21 2523 5125
Email: Ana.Fonseca@umusic.com
www.wccm.com.br

**Canada**
Christian Meditation Community National Resource Centre
PO Box 552, Station NDG
Montreal
Quebec H4A 3P9
Canada
Tel: +1 514 485 7928
Fax: +1 514 489 9899
Email: ChristianMeditation@bellnet.ca
www.meditatio.ca

Méditation chretiénne du Québec
7400 boul. St Laurent, Suite 513
Montréal
Québec H2R 2Y1
Canada
Tel: +1 514 525 4649
Fax: +1 514 525 8110
Email: medchre@bellnet.ca
www.meditatio.ca

**France**
Communauté Mondiale de Méditants Chrétiens
126 rue Pelleport
75020 Paris
France
Tel: 33 1 40 31 89 73
Email: cmmc@wanadoo.fr
www.meditationchretienne.org

**Germany**
Zentrum für Christliche Meditation
Untere Leiten 12d
82065 Baierbrunn
Tel: +49 (0)89/680 209 14
Email: mariya@wccm.de
www.wccm.de

**India**
Christian Meditation Centre
Kripa Foundation
Mt Carmel Church
81/A Chapel Road
Bandra (W)
Mumbai 400050
India
Tel: +91 22 640 5411
Fax: +91 22 643 9296
Email: frjoe@bom5.vsnl.net.in

**Ireland**
Christian Meditation Centre
4 Eblana Avenue
Dun Laoghaire
Co. Dublin
Ireland
Tel: +353 1 280 1505

Fax: +353 1 280 8720
Email: mclougf@hotmail.com
www.wccmireland.org

## Italy
Comunità Mondiale per la Meditazione Cristiana
Via Marche, 2/a
25125 Brescia
Italy
Tel: +39 030 224549
Email: wccmitalia@virgilio.it
www.meditazionecristiana.org

## Mexico
La Communidad Mundial de Meditacion Cristiana
Paseo de Golondrinas Closter 11-401
C.P. 40880
Ixtapa, Guerrero
Mexico
Ubifone: 800-1320 1320
Tel: +52 755 55 3 01 20
Email: lucia_gayon@yahoo.com
www.meditacioncristiana.com

## New Zealand
Christian Meditation Community
PO Box 15-402
Tauranga
New Zealand
Tel: +64 7 544 7955
Email: stanman@xtra.co.nz

**Singapore**
Christian Meditation Centre
Church of the Holy Family
6 Chapel Road
Singapore 429509
Tel: +65 67376279
Email: daulet@pacific.net.sg
Tel: +65 64458062
Email: rebeccalim@pacific.net.sg
www.wccm.org/singapor.html

**United Kingdom**
London Christian Meditation Centre
St Mark's
Myddelton Square
London
EC1R 1XX
Tel: +44 20 7833 9615
Fax: +44 20 7713 6346
Email: uk@wccm.org
www.christian-meditation.org.uk

**USA**
WCCM US National Information Center
627 N 6th Avenue
Tucson
Arizona 85705-8330
USA
Tel: +1 800 324 8305 / +1 520 882 0290
Fax: +1 520 882 0311
E-mail: meditate@mediomedia.com
www.wccm-usa.org

For countries not listed above, please contact the International Centre.